EASY RAMBLES

AROUND
AMBLESIDE & GRASMERE

VIVIENNE CROW

QUESTA

ISBN 978-1-898808-27-5

Maps:
The maps accompanying the walks in this book are purely
diagrammatic, and are based on maps produced by Harvey Maps
(Licence No. 75930 © Harvey Map Services Ltd.)

Published by
Questa Publishing Limited
27 Camwood, Clayton-le-Woods,
Bamber Bridge,
Lancashire PR5 8LA

CONTENTS

NOTE

No attempt has been made to grade the walks in this book, as this is too subjective, but they are in ascending order of difficulty. Use the information about distance and height gain to calculate how long the walk will take.

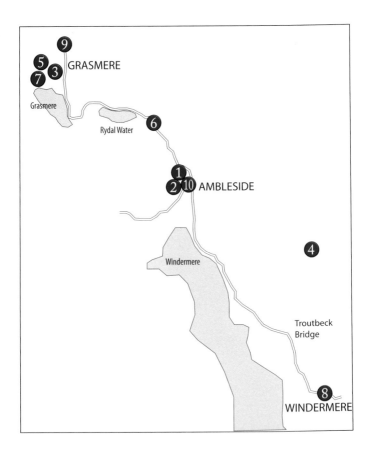

INTRODUCTION

One of the many great joys of the Lake District is that you don't have to climb to the tops of the highest fells to appreciate the wonderful scenery or get the best views. You don't even need to walk many miles before you've left the busy towns and villages behind.

The area around Grasmere and Ambleside is no exception to this. Moody tarns poised majestically on the lip of secluded corries, breathtaking vistas that will literally stop you in your tracks, atmospheric lakes, awesome waterfalls and wild, lonely valleys – they are all visited on the walks in this book. And with every step taken, the area's rich and colourful history makes it presence felt – from the Romans to some of the Lake District's most famous former residents, including William Wordsworth and Beatrix Potter.

The creation of the National Park and the conservation of the landscape, both natural and manmade, owes a great deal to these and other local writers.

Wordsworth adored the Lakes, particularly the area around Grasmere and Rydal where he lived for much of his adult life, and his poetry is clearly inspired by this passion and his love of nature. During his lifetime, he became a staunch defender of the region, trying to protect it from the intrusion of the railway and other developments that he felt threatened its unique beauty and serenity. He described the Lakes as "a sort of national property in which every man has a right and interest who has an eye to perceive and a heart to enjoy". His ideas didn't become a reality until 1949 when the National Parks were created, the Lake District becoming the second in 1951.

Although born in London, Beatrix Potter's love of the countryside stemmed from her childhood holidays in the Lakes. As a young woman, she became friends with Canon Hardwicke Rawnsley, one of the co-founders of the National Trust, and his views on the need to protect the natural beauty of the Lakes had a profound effect on the writer. She eventually moved to the area and gained the respect of local people as a top breeder of Herdwick sheep, the Lake District's own, hardy breed. When she died in 1943, she left 14 Lakeland farms

– a total of 4,000 acres – to the National Trust.

Farming continues to play a significant role today. As you wander up the Trout Beck valley, where Beatrix Potter reared one of her famous Herdwick flocks, or along the old Corspe Road from Grasmere to Rydal, you can't fail to notice the hedgerows and drystone walls that adorn these valleys. Climb up to Lily Tarn or on to the grassy summit of Silver How and chances are that you'll come across the sheep that graze these fells, keeping them clear of dense vegetation.

Although farming plays a major role in conserving the pastoral landscape that generations of tourists have come to love, it is the natural forces of volcanic activity, sedimentary processes and glaciation that initially moulded and then shaped these magnificent fells and valleys.

The Lake District is essentially a massive volcanic dome fissured by tectonic forces and then sculpted by huge rivers of ice to create a spray of valleys and dividing mountain ranges radiating from a central hub like spokes from a wheel.

In the north are some of the oldest mountains in the world, composed of Skiddaw slates laid down more than 450 million years ago. These give us steep, smooth, rounded fells, but further south, the Borrowdale volcanics lend themselves to a rougher, more angular landscape. A thin band of limestone, known as Coniston limestone, separates these volcanics from the softer, sedimentary rocks of the south, known as the Silurian series. These give rise to the soft, rolling hills around Windermere and Kendal.

Walk any of the paths in this book, especially if you are up with the dawn or out for an evening saunter, and there is a good chance you will encounter some of the local wildlife. High fell fauna include foxes, hares and stoats. Herds of red deer can often be seen above the treeline, while the woods are home to badgers, roe deer, voles, shrews, occasional otters and the iconic red squirrel, sadly under threat from the incursion of the more dominant American greys into one of their last bastions in England.

The birds that make the fell-tops their home all year round include ravens, buzzards and peregrines. Lower down, in the spring, you'll encounter migratory species such as redstart, pied flycatcher, wood warbler and tree pipit as well as the year-round residents, including chaffinch, green and great-spotted woodpeckers, nuthatch and sparrowhawk. You can find waterfowl on Grasmere, Rydal Water and Windermere, while the lively rivers and becks are home to dippers, wagtails and common sandpipers.

The walking routes are roughly in ascending order of difficulty. Some keep to the valley floor, following idyllic farm and lakeshore paths, while others head up to secluded tarns or on to the easily accessible tops of low-lying fells such as Helm Crag, Orrest Head and Wansfell Pike.

On foot, taking in the surroundings at a slow, even pace, you cannot help but be moved by the area around Grasmere and Ambleside just as poets, writers and conservationists have been for generations. It is, in the words of Thomas Gray, "one of the sweetest landscapes that art ever attempted to imitate".

1

SCANDALE
& HIGH SWEDEN BRIDGE

Scandale is the narrow valley squeezed between the eastern arm of the popular Fairfield Horseshoe walk and the ridge that culminates in Red Screes. Despite having a clear drove road running straight through it, it feels like a wild place. Using mostly well-walked paths and clear tracks, this short stroll climbs very gradually to provide just a tiny, teasing taste of the valley. The return route crosses humpback High Sweden Bridge to follow Scandale Beck as it plunges dramatically – and rather noisily – into a steep-sided gorge.

> **Start/Finish:** Rydal Road car park in Ambleside,
> just north of village centre on A591 (NY374047)
> **Distance:** 5km (3.1 miles)
> **Height gain:** 238m (780ft)

1. Use the pedestrian bridge near the toilet block to exit the car park. Turn left along the main road and then immediately right up Smithy Brow towards the Kirkstone Pass. Take the first turning on your left and, when the narrow lane forks, keep left – along Nook Lane.

2. Follow the surfaced lane until it ends at Nook End Farm. Walk into the farmyard and then out through the double green gates at the other end. Keep to the left-hand track beyond the gates; this soon crosses Scandale Beck via Low Sweden Bridge.

> *The name Sweden, which crops up several times in the lower reaches of Scandale, is thought to be a corruption of the dialect word 'swithen', meaning land cleared by burning.*

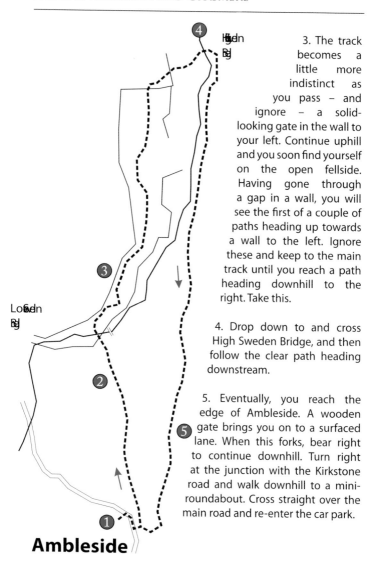

3. The track becomes a little more indistinct as you pass – and ignore – a solid-looking gate in the wall to your left. Continue uphill and you soon find yourself on the open fellside. Having gone through a gap in a wall, you will see the first of a couple of paths heading up towards a wall to the left. Ignore these and keep to the main track until you reach a path heading downhill to the right. Take this.

4. Drop down to and cross High Sweden Bridge, and then follow the clear path heading downstream.

5. Eventually, you reach the edge of Ambleside. A wooden gate brings you on to a surfaced lane. When this forks, bear right to continue downhill. Turn right at the junction with the Kirkstone road and walk downhill to a mini-roundabout. Cross straight over the main road and re-enter the car park.

9

2

LILY TARN

Lily Tarn, located about 200m above sea level, is hidden on low-lying fells to the west of Ambleside. This short walk takes a roundabout route to reach it, visiting a wonderful, surprise viewpoint of Windermere along the way. It's easy to get lost among the maze of paths up here, but things become a lot easier when you reach the clear path at the base of Loughrigg. This walk is best saved for a bright summer's evening when you can watch the sun setting behind Crinkle Crags.

Start/Finish: Rydal Road car park in Ambleside, just north of village centre on A591 (NY374047)
Distance: 5.3km (3.3 miles)
Height gain: 207m (680ft)

1. Use the pedestrian bridge near the toilet block to exit the car park and turn right along the main road, bearing right when it forks. Take the first turning on the right, just after the cinema, and turn left immediately – towards Loughrigg and Rothay Park. Pass St Mary's Parish Church on your left and then walk straight across the park.

2. Cross one bridge and then go over the humpback bridge over the River Rothay. Turn right along the quiet lane and then, about 50 metres beyond the cattle grid, turn left through a kissing-gate beside another cattle grid.

3. Climb the winding, surfaced lane for about 400 metres and then, at a sharp bend to the right, leave it by crossing a stone stile in the wall on your left – signposted Clappersgate.

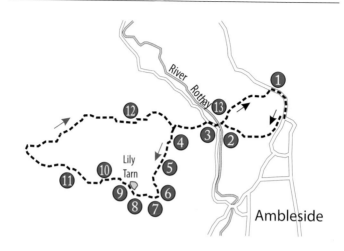

4. Leaving the woods, the path crosses a narrow footbridge and then forks. Bear right and then, at the top of the few steps, bear left along a muddy trail that soon joins a clearer path coming in from the right.

5. The path climbs alongside a tiny beck for a short while and then swings sharp left. Don't be tempted by the faint path off to the right here. In fact, don't be tempted by any paths to the right; keep to the mostly level path for now.

6. Suddenly, you are stopped in your tracks as the ground ahead drops away and the northern end of Windermere is revealed in all its glittering glory.

> *Windermere is far from being the most scenic of the lakes, but this is a lovely view, made all the better by its unexpectedness. Just to the east of where the river enters the lake, you should be able to make out the remains of the Roman fort, Galava. At the centre of the fort stood three main buildings – the granary, the commandant's*

house and the Principia, or headquarters. It was manned by 500 auxiliary troops and was often attacked by local tribes. Evidence from coins and pottery suggest Galava was inhabited until late into the 4th century, at about the time that the Romans were withdrawing from Hadrian's Wall.

The Roman legions first entered the far north-west of England in about 71AD, when Petillius Cerialis began to crush the Brigantes, the Celtic people who dominated the region at the time. Agricola then managed to push north from Chester to Carlisle in 78AD and placed garrisons between the Solway Firth and the River Tyne. Although the Romans were soon clearly in charge and made allegiances with the Brigantes, the ancient Britons weren't truly quashed until about 140AD.

Although there is little trace of three centuries of Roman rule in local place-names or the Cumbrian dialect, the impression left upon the landscape by the occupation is clear to see. From around 120AD, a system of roads was built, including High Street, the highest Roman road in the country, which runs for 25 miles across the eastern fells from the Roman fort Brocavum at Brougham, near Penrith to Galava. Cumbria is also dotted with the remains of forts, milecastles, marching camps, bath-houses and, of course, the magnificent Hadrian's Wall. Created on the orders of the Emperor Hadrian, work on the wall began in 122AD. It ran from Bowness-on-Solway to Wallsend on the Tyne estuary.

7. When you can tear yourself away from the view, you will see that the path, now just a faint line through the grass, swings right along this tiny ridge of high ground until it reaches a wall. Bear right to walk uphill with the wall on your immediate left.

8. Cross the ladder stile and bear half-right – you can either climb on

to the little craggy knoll here for some more views of Windermere and Ambleside, or you can swing round the northern side of it. Either way, you soon find yourself confronted by a confusing jumble of paths – simply aim for the highest of the rocky outcrops about 200 metres to the west. At the base of this, tucked away in a dip and hidden from view, is a tiny pond, a delightful little pool of water. Lily Tarn is just a stone's throw away now. Simply make your way to the western side of this first pond and then turn right along the path.

9. When you find Lily Tarn, keep to the wall side of the water. Things get a little boggy around the outlet stream. It's probably best to head right up to the water's edge and use the few rocks there as stepping stones.

10. The path heads mostly W now – in the general direction of Crinkle Crags in the distance. Keep to the clearest path at all times, following the line of the wall which is a little way over to the left at first. As you regain the wall, the path swings more NW and drops down to and through a kissing-gate.

11. Don't be tempted by any paths up to the right on to the higher ground – keep following the line of the wall until you reach a small beck. Cross this, climb the slope on the other side and then turn right along the clear path at the base of Loughrigg. You quickly ford the beck again and the path climbs briefly before starting to drop.

12. The track eventually becomes a surfaced lane that winds its way back down to the quiet lane alongside which the River Rothay runs. Turn right along the lane and then left over the humpback bridge.

13. You could now retrace your steps to the car park via the park. Alternatively, go through the metal gate immediately after the humpback bridge and follow the surfaced pathway until you reach a residential street. Turn left along this and then right at the main road to return to the car park.

3

GRASMERE & RYDAL WATER

Grasmere and Rydal are at the very heart of Wordsworth country. It sometimes seems that every building, every inch of land and every single daffodil has links with the Cockermouth-born poet and his family. This walk follows quiet lanes and pleasant tracks from his burial place in Grasmere and past two of his homes to the tiny village of Rydal. It then returns along the shores of the two small, but perfectly formed lakes – Rydal Water and Grasmere. There are a few short climbs on the route, but nothing too taxing; and the paths are generally well-signposted and easy to follow.

> **Start/Finish:** The parish church of St Oswald's
> in Grasmere village (NY306225)
> **Distance:** 8.5km (5.3 miles)
> **Height gain:** 208m (683ft)

1. From the church porch, walk out on to the road and turn left, gradually heading out of Grasmere.

> *William Wordsworth and various members of his family – including sister Dorothy, wife Mary, daughter Dora and son William – are buried in the churchyard at St Oswald's.*

2. At a small roundabout, turn right on to the A591 and then immediately left on to a minor road.

> *You soon pass Dove Cottage, where Wordsworth and his sister Dorothy lived from 1799 until 1808. Built in the 1600s, it was originally an inn called the Dove and Olive Branch. The building has been open to visitors since*

1899 and still houses much of the Wordsworths' original furniture.

3. As you continue to climb gently uphill on the quiet, asphalted lane, the next interesting feature you see is the Coffin Stone, a large rock just to the left of the road.

This road and the pleasant track that you follow as far as Rydal used to be known as the Corpse Road. Before St Mary's Church in Ambleside was consecrated, coffins had to be transported along this route from Ambleside to St Oswald's Church in Grasmere for interment. The Coffin Stone (also known as the Resting Stone) was used to support the coffin while the bearers rested.

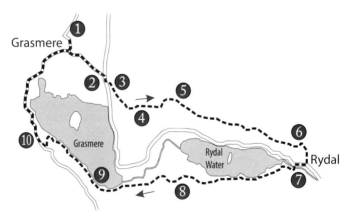

4. Just after passing a lane and then a small pond on the left, you reach a fork. Bear left towards Alcock Tarn, climbing more steeply now. Ignoring one track to the left (to Alcock Tarn) and another to the right (to White Moss), keep following the surfaced lane. You pass three secluded slate cottages, the last of which is called Dunnabeck. Beyond here, the lane becomes a rough track.

5. Follow the track in and out of pretty woodland and across grazing land with views down to Rydal Water. There are a few benches along this stretch of the path, so you can rest and enjoy the scenery.

6. Eventually you reach a quiet lane, along which you turn right.

As you head downhill, you pass Rydal Mount, which was Wordsworth's home from 1813 until he died in 1850. He moved here to escape from the memories associated with Grasmere after two of his children died. He had also recently secured the post of distributor of stamps for Westmorland, a post with an annual salary of £300, so the family could afford something a little more stylish. Like all his homes though, this one was rented – it belonged to the Le Flemings of Rydal Hall. Wordsworth did, however, own a patch of ground behind the church and had intended to build a home for his daughter Dora on it. After she died in 1847, he planted hundreds of daffodils there in her memory. The site, Dora's Field, is now in the care of the National Trust.

Continuing further down the lane, you pass the entrance to Rydal Hall on your left. This building, which originally belonged to the Le Fleming family, dates from the 17th century, although the front is Victorian. At the beginning of the 20th century, the landscape architect, Thomas Mawson, was commissioned to create a series of Italianate terraces sweeping down from the main house. Work on restoring the gardens began in 2005. The hall and grounds now form part of a conference centre and retreat run by the Carlisle Diocese.

The tiny church at the bottom of the lane is St Mary's, built in 1824. Needless to say, this also has a Wordsworth link – he played a role in its design and was church warden here for a while. The Wordsworth family pew was the one in front of the lectern.

7. Turn right along the main road and, when you reach the Badger Bar, cross the road and go through the gap in the wall. Cross the River Rothay via the wooden footbridge and then turn right to head upstream. You soon find yourself beside Rydal Water. Keep to the path nearest the water as it winds its way through woodland.

8. Beyond the western end of the lake, with bracken-covered slopes leading up to the crag-crowned top of Loughrigg on your left, you begin to climb alongside a drystone wall. Ignore all paths off until you crest the rise and get your first glimpse of the bottom end of Grasmere. Bear right here, downhill, following a path that quickly drops to the shores of Grasmere.

9. Walk along the shingle beach and through a gate to enter some woodland. Follow the main path as it hugs the shore. After about three-quarters-of-a-mile of lakeside walking, it suddenly bends sharp left, away from the water. It climbs to a gate at the road, near some large slate villas.

10. Turn right along the road and follow it for almost a mile, back to the church where the walk started.

DAFFODILS

Not all of the daffodils you see in the Lake District are of the wild variety about which Wordsworth famously waxed so lyrical. The native Narcissus pseudonarcissus is a more delicate and graceful plant than its cultivated cousin. It can be identified by its pale yellow outer petals surrounding a golden-yellow trumpet. Its strap-like, upright, grey-green leaves are also distinctive. Wild daffodils are generally found on moist banks in open oak or ash woods. Cultivated daffodils, on the other hand, are twice as big as the wild variety and considerably more hardy, having been raised to survive in colder conditions.

4

TROUTBECK

Walkers looking for the Lake District idyll need go no further than Troutbeck. Drystone walls snake up and down the western side of the verdant valley, dissecting the rolling farmland into small enclosures, and the area is dotted with pretty cottages worthy of many a chocolate box top. On the eastern side is a line of rugged fells, part of the Kentmere Horseshoe. Could there be anywhere more perfect on a sunny day when the sound of birdsong fills the trees? And the easy walking along lanes, tracks and farm paths on this route is so straightforward that you'll have plenty of opportunity to appreciate it.

Start/Finish: Small parking area near Troutbeck village
on a lane just off the A592, 120 metres south
of the parish church (NY412027)
Distance: 8.9km (5.5 miles)
Height gain: 219m (717ft)

---

1. Turn right along the lane and then left at the main road. Immediately after passing the church, turn left along the public bridleway. As you draw level with a white gate in the churchyard wall on your left, cross the wooden stile beside the gate to your right. The path follows the line of the fence on the right for a short while and then climbs a low embankment and goes through two kissing-gates in quick succession.

2. At a fingerpost at a crossing of tracks, turn right. Cross straight over the main road and down the bridleway on the other side.

3. When you reach a surfaced lane, turn right towards Kentmere Park. This lane winds its way along the valley bottom, crossing two bridges

along the way, always in the general direction of Troutbeck Tongue and Troutbeck Park.

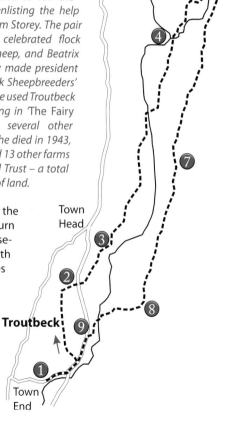

> *Beatrix Potter bought the 1,900-acre sheep farm, Troutbeck Park, in 1923. Before long, she decided to run the farm herself, enlisting the help of shepherd Tom Storey. The pair established a celebrated flock of Herdwick sheep, and Beatrix was eventually made president of the Herdwick Sheepbreeders' Association. She used Troutbeck Park as a setting in 'The Fairy Caravan' and several other pieces. When she died in 1943, she left this and 13 other farms to the National Trust – a total of 4,000 acres of land.*

4. Immediately after the second bridge, turn right across the close-cropped grass. The path isn't obvious – it passes to the right of a small mound in the middle of the field and then uphill towards a gate in a drystone wall. Beyond the gate, turn right along the rough track.

19

5. Immediately after going through the second of the next two gates, turn sharp right to go through another gate and cross the beck via a plank bridge near a stone barn. Once across the beck, head uphill for a few strides and then bear right along a level, grassy track; don't follow the track up into the disused quarry.

6. At a double gate in a few hundred metres, make sure you go through the higher of the two. If in any doubt about the route of the bridleway, simply follow the wall on your right. The only time you lose the wall is at a wide ford near a large stone barn – and beyond this point, the track becomes obvious anyway.

7. Follow the track all the way to Long Green Head and then go through the gate just to the left of the farm buildings. Continue along the track, again with the wall on your right.

> *You are following the course of Trout Beck, as you did on the route out, but now from a better vantage point, slightly higher up the valley side. From here, you get a better sense of the many enclosures that fill the western side of the dale. This area is marked on maps as "The Hundreds". Troutbeck's common pastures were once divided into three "Hundreds" – the Upper, Middle and Lower. Each Hundred originally comprised 100 hides, the amount of land regarded as enough to support a peasant family. By the 19th century, each Hundred had to maintain one bull, one constable and one bridge. From this a saying sprung up in neighbouring valleys: "There's three hundred bridges i'Troutbeck, three hundred bulls, three hundred constables and many hundred feuls (fools)".*

8. Having walked 1.2km from Long Green Head Farm, you reach a fork in the track. Bear right to head downhill and into the Limefitt caravan site. When you reach the big, white house, follow the public bridleway signpost that directs you along the main driveway and off the site, crossing Trout Beck along the way.

9. Turn left along the main road, and the parking area is down the first turning on the right after the church.

> *There has been a church on the site of today's Jesus Church since the 16th century. The whole building was dismantled and rebuilt in 1736, and major alterations took place in 1861. The large east window is the combined work of Edward Burne-Jones, William Morris and Ford Madox Brown. The local story is that the latter two were in Troutbeck on a fishing holiday when Burne-Jones was working on the window, and they stayed to help him.*

DRYSTONE WALLS

Drystone walls are an integral part of the Cumbrian landscape – creating the small enclosures that are so typical of Lakeland valleys, and running for seemingly endless miles on the open fell-tops. Built without mortar or cement, some of them date back to the late 13th century when the Cistercian monks of Furness Abbey farmed the region, but most were built during the Enclosure movement of the 18th and 19th centuries.

The walls are built on a foundation of two parallel rows of large boulders on either side of a trench. The sides are then built up and the inside is filled with smaller stones. At regular intervals, a layer of 'throughstones' is placed across the entire width of the wall to strengthen it. Walls tend to be wider at the bottom than at the top – for stability. They are generally topped with a row of slanting or vertical stones, known as 'cam-stones', to discourage sheep from climbing over the wall.

5

EASEDALE TARN

Easedale Tarn is one of the Lake District's most visited tarns and it's hardly surprising. The tarn itself is in a lovely location with steep, rocky faces to the north. The walk up passes close to the dramatic waterfalls of Sourmilk Gill and the return route is via the peaceful Far Easedale. The paths are rough underfoot in places and the climb up to the tarn is moderately steep, but it isn't especially long.

The only difficulty you are likely to experience is when you try to cross the stream at the western end of the tarn – if the water level is too high, simply retrace your steps to the other end of the tarn and cross via the stepping stones in the outlet stream. This will mean missing out the path around the northern side of the tarn, but, if the stream is too high, then you can guarantee that the ground on the north-western side of the tarn will be extremely boggy.

Start/Finish: The beginning of Easedale Road in Grasmere village (NY337076) – opposite the Sam Read book shop
Distance: 9km (5.6 miles)
Height gain: 300m (984ft)

---

1. From the village centre, walk along Easedale Road for nearly 700 metres until you see a small footbridge in the trees to your left. Turn left to cross this bridge – signposted Easedale Tarn – and then a second, smaller bridge. Although rough underfoot, the track ahead, with Easedale Beck on your right, is easy to follow.

As you walk upstream, don't be tempted by the bridge on your right or the gate with the yellow waymarker to your left; simply stick to the clear, beckside track until it goes through a gate. Beyond this gate, cross the farm track and keep straight ahead on a narrower path – a signpost, partly hidden in a holly bush on the right, shows the way.

2. The path veers away from the beck for a short while and then regains it. After a kissing-gate, the more sustained climbing begins – on a constructed path running alongside a drystone wall and then beside the tumultuous waterfalls of Sourmilk Gill.

3. When you reach the tarn, turn right to drop down to the outlet stream, which can be easily crossed via stepping stones, and then head downhill. Alternatively, those wishing to complete the whole walk – and who don't mind potentially getting their feet wet – can follow the 2km circuit of the tarn.

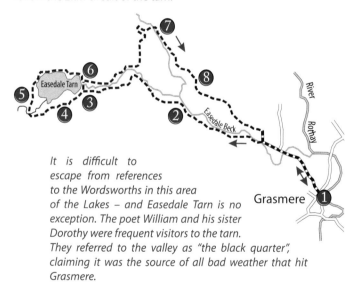

It is difficult to escape from references to the Wordsworths in this area of the Lakes – and Easedale Tarn is no exception. The poet William and his sister Dorothy were frequent visitors to the tarn. They referred to the valley as "the black quarter", claiming it was the source of all bad weather that hit Grasmere.

In Victorian times, there used to be a refreshments hut up here, serving light lunches and hot drinks to the well-dressed, middle-class tourists who toiled up from the valley below. There was even a small boat for hire on the tarn. If you look just to the left of the main path, you will see a large boulder with some smaller stones to the right of it. The large boulder formed part of one wall of the hut. The smaller stones are all that remain of the base of the structure.

4. For the tarn circuit, follow the clear path around the southern side of the water. As you draw level with the western end of the tarn, you can turn right along a faint, grassy path to cross the inlet stream at the tarn's edge. This tends to be extremely boggy, so it may be better to continue for another 250 metres or so – until you see a small, solitary tree about 50 metres ahead of you to the right of the main path. Now head down the bank to cross the flat, boggy area below. There is a path on the ground, but it is faint. To avoid soggy feet, keep to the slightly higher ground to the left as much as possible. Ford the beck that feeds the tarn, but be careful because the rocks on the stream bed are very slippery.

5. You now need to pick up the path that runs around the northern edge of the tarn. There are many faint paths to choose from at first as you cross more boggy ground, but eventually you should reach a clear, mostly dry path close to the water's edge. You'll pick this up near a small, walled enclosure.

6. When you reach the tarn's outlet stream, those who decided against the detour rejoin the main route as it descends with the beck on the right – using stepping stones for the wettest sections. About 700 metres beyond the tarn, you lose the beck as the path starts descending into Far Easedale. It is hard to go wrong here – the path is clear, there are yellow waymarkers to guide you and, just in case you are in any doubt, there is a huge boulder with "Grasmere" and a large white arrow painted on it.

7. Cross the wooden footbridge in the valley bottom and then turn right to follow the beck downstream. This is a lovely spot to linger for

a while – trees overhang the small gorge where crystal clear waters tumble over the smooth rocks; a stark contrast to the noisy, white-water cascades of Sourmilk Gill.

8. You eventually lose this beck, but the track ahead is clear. At a junction of tracks, ignore the turning on the left and continue towards Grasmere. Go through the gate and head down the lane and on to an asphalt road. Turn left and follow the quiet road back into the village.

> The village of Grasmere used to play an important role in the woollen industry. By the middle of the 15th century, the parish of Grasmere, which included Rydal, Langdale and Loughrigg, had six fulling mills. This number had risen to 18 by the 16th century. The mills dressed and finished the Herdwick wool for the markets in Kendal. Lakeland was an ideal place for the industry, not only because of the local sheep and the proximity of fast-flowing becks to operate the wheels of the mills, but also because a number of plants growing on the fells could be used to dye the cloth. Green bracken fronds, when burned, also provided a supply of potash which, when mixed with tallow, formed a soap to wash the wool.

6

AROUND THE BASE OF LOUGHRIGG

After a short climb up from a quiet lane, this becomes a relatively gentle walk around the base of Loughrigg Fell, along clear, easy-to-follow paths. There are a few other uphill sections, but these are mostly short and well spaced out. Take your time and enjoy the wonderful views which change with every turn on this circuit. As you climb to the south-east of the fell, it is Fairfield which dominates the scene. The top of the ascent provides a brilliant view of Windermere to the south. Then, as you round Ivy Crag at the far southern tip of Loughrigg, the Langdale Pikes suddenly appear in all their splendour. As if that wasn't enough, the return route on the northern side of the fell passes high above the serene lakes of Grasmere and Rydal Water.

Start/Finish: Pelter Bridge car park, near Rydal (NY364059)
Distance: 9.3km (5.8 miles)
Height gain: 317m (1,040ft)

---

1. Turn right out of the car park and head downhill to a T-junction. Turn right again and follow the road as it winds its way towards Ambleside, beside the River Rothay. Do not be tempted by a footpath on your right, signposted Loughrigg Fell, after 850 metres.

> *This declined shortcut on to Loughrigg Fell leads up past Fox Ghyll, a 17th century house that was the home of Thomas de Quincey from 1820. He moved here with his wife, a local farmer's daughter, from Dove Cottage, which he had been renting since the Wordsworths moved out. His famous autobiographical novel* Confessions of an English Opium-Eater *was published in 1822.*

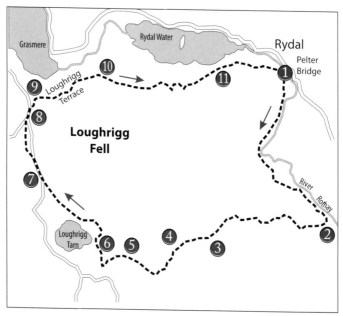

2. Having walked 2km from the parking area, turn right to cross a cattle grid with a public bridleway fingerpost beside it. This surfaced track heads fairly steeply uphill at first, but the gradient eases soon after passing a small group of homes on the right.

> *The track goes through several gates as it continues gently uphill. Soon after passing a secluded house on the right – as you gain more open land – a gap in the wall on the right provides a chance to look across to the Fairfield Horseshoe. After a third gate, the views to the west start opening out – with Wetherlam appearing straight ahead.*

3. The track soon descends to a small beck, which can be crossed by

stepping stones. Immediately after crossing, ignore the path off to the right; keep to the clear track.

4. The path now starts to descend, soon running alongside a drystone wall on the left. The bracken-covered slopes to your right belong to Loughrigg. When the path splits, take the left branch down to a large gate from where you can see Skelwith Bridge. Do not go through the gate; instead, stick with the level path around the base of the fell. The magnificent view ahead is of the Langdale Pikes.

5. Go through a gate and head downhill on the loose, stony track. About 200 metres beyond the gate, watch out for two gates close to each other on the right. Go through the second one. (It has a 'footpath' and 'no cycling' sign on it.) Walking to the left of a group of beech trees, cross the small field and climb the stile at the other side.

6. Walk briefly with the fence on your right before the faint path begins heading downhill – Loughrigg Tarn here acting as the perfect foreground for many holiday snaps of the Langdales. Cross the wooden step stile in the iron railings and turn right along the gravel lane.

It is Loughrigg Tarn that gives the fell to the east its name, Loughrigg meaning 'ridge above the lake'.

7. When you reach a road, go through the gate and turn right. Walk along the asphalt for about 400 metres and then turn left through a wooden gate into a small area of attractive woodland. The gravel path soon splits; bear right here along the narrower branch to walk gently uphill. Turn right at the top of this path to climb a couple of steps and then leave the woodland via a metal gate.

8. Turn left along the road and then go through the gate on your right into Deer Bolts Wood. This clear, wide track is soon joined by another as you drop to a metal kissing-gate, which provides access to open land again.

9. Ignore the path heading steeply uphill on the right and walk along Loughrigg Terrace, high above Grasmere. There are plenty of opportunities to sit and admire the view of the lake on one of the many benches along this stretch of the walk.

10. Take the next clear path on the right, heading gently uphill at first. Bear right at a junction with a wider track. The lake down to the left now is Rydal Water.

> *The track makes its way to the higher of the Rydal Caves – which was closed at the time of writing due to a rockfall – and then winds its way down to the lower cave.*
>
> *The caves are manmade, a result of slate quarrying. The small pool in the mouth of the top cave is home to some tiny fish which are said to be the descendants of stock placed there by visiting schoolchildren.*

11. Keep to the wide track, going through a gate just after you are joined by another track coming up from the left. The track eventually goes over to asphalt and drops back down to the Pelter Bridge car park.

7

SILVER HOW

Seen from Grasmere, the craggy, eastern slopes of Silver How make this relatively little fell seem much higher than its mere 394 metres. And when you're on its summit, although an uninspiring place in itself, you can be forgiven for thinking you're on a much grander mountain as you peruse the impressive Lakeland panorama. The low-lying fells in this area are very popular, so there are paths all over the place. You'll need to pay close attention to the walk description, and a compass may come in handy to confirm you're on the correct route. There are a number of short but steep climbs as well as some road walking, but much of the route is on pleasant, grassy paths.

Start/Finish: Red Bank Road car park near the Grasmere Garden Centre in Grasmere village (NY336073)
Distance: 6.6km (4.1 miles)
Height gain: 359m (1,177ft)

---

1. Leave the car park and turn left along the road. After three-quarters of a mile, turn right up a track opposite a bungalow with a post-box set into its wall – signposted Loughrigg Terrace and Great Langdale.

> *This track was not only a packhorse route, but also a corpse road by which people from Langdale were brought for burial in Grasmere until about 1821 when consecrated ground was created in Langdale.*

2. At a junction of paths near a bench, ignore the metal gate on your left and keep straight ahead – towards Elterwater and Langdale. You'll see two wooden gates here; go through the one on the left, with the

yellow waymarker on it. The path climbs steadily with a drystone wall to the left at first and then plateaus out just beyond a small gate.

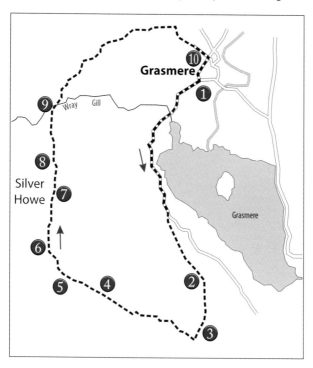

3. Soon after going through the gate, the wall on your right turns sharply to ascend the fell with a faint footpath beside it. Ignore this path; instead, continue for another 15 metres to take the next path on your right. This climbs steeply, emerging just to the left of a tiny tarn. You are now on a gorgeous, low-level ridge path that undulates through bracken and rocky outcrops.

4. About 400 metres after gaining the ridge, cross straight over a

grassy track running north-south and clamber up to a cairn-topped summit for your first uninterrupted view of the Langdales.

5. Continuing along the ridge, you cross a damp depression on stepping stones where you ignore a cairned path off to the left. Beyond, climb easily on grass, keeping to a clear path to the right of the high ground. About 250 metres before you reach some more rugged looking terrain, the path splits. Bear left and you soon pass a large cairn on your right. Immediately after it, you swing left to head uphill on a well-walked track and, in another 50 metres, turn right to climb more steeply.

6. When the gradient eases, make your way over to the large cairn on the edge of the fell to your right. From here, head north along a barely perceptible path that drops down into a small bowl and then climbs out of it to meet a wide, grassy path. Turn right and climb gently across the southern flank of the fell. With higher ground to your left, the slopes to your right drop away steeply with good views down to the small lakes of Grasmere and Rydal Water.

7. Don't be tempted by any paths to the left. Eventually, you reach the highest point on Silver How, marked by a rather pathetic-looking cairn on top of a rocky outcrop. The views from up here are pretty amazing, especially to the east where Fairfield and the Helvellyn range dominate.

8. The beginning of the onward path can be difficult to find, although it is easy to follow once you are on it. If you stand on the northern edge of the high ground, you should be able to see it snaking steeply down the fellside – it starts just to the left of the cairn. Ignoring a faint path off to the right as you descend, drop down and cross a stream at the base of the steep slope. The path, now heading north, becomes fainter as it crosses damp ground, but there are cairns to guide you.

9. Ignoring one faint path off to the right along the way, you eventually drop down into the steep-sided, tree-lined gorge of Wray Gill and,

having crossed the beck, turn right. Join a wider path coming in from the left to descend through an area of juniper and then down to a wall corner. Keep the wall on your right and then go through a kissing-gate to walk between two drystone walls. Turn right along a surfaced lane near an old farmhouse.

> *As you head along this surfaced lane, you will see a large house up to the right. This is Allan Bank, the home of William Wordsworth and his family from 1808 to 1811. The poet once described the building as the "temple of abomination", because he felt it spoiled the view of Grasmere. They moved here when his wife Mary was expecting their fourth child and Dove Cottage became too small for the growing family.*

10. At a junction of roads in the village, take the first turning on the right. This road leads back to the car park.

Norse influence

Pick up any map of the Lake District and you will find it awash with words not unlike those on any modern map of Norway or Iceland – words such as fell (fjell), beck (bekkr), tarn (tjörn) and dale (dalr). It is generally believed that the first Norse settlers came into the area, not directly from Scandinavia, but via Ireland and the Isle of Man some time before the second half of the 9th century. Remnants of the old Norse in place names in the Grasmere and Ambleside area include Orrest Head – the place where a battle (orrusta) took place – and Ambleside iself, meaning Hamal's saeter, or summer pasture.

8

ORREST HEAD & BEYOND

*For some walkers, little Orrest Head (238m) with its fantastic all-round
views is an end in itself, but this outing takes you beyond the popular
top and out along the lonely Dubbs Road to a high point of 279m.
Having left Windermere behind long ago, you get a surprising sense of
remoteness as you gaze wistfully into the beautiful Trout Beck valley
from this vantage point.*

*The walk up to Orrest Head is relatively gentle and afterwards easier still.
There are paths across farmland, which are generally well signposted,
and a few short sections along quiet country roads.*

> **Start/Finish:** Windermere Railway Station
> **Distance:** 11.3km (7 miles)
> **Height gain:** 316m (1,036ft)

1. Turn left out of the railway station building and then, at the
complicated junction where the station driveway meets the A591,
carefully cross to the north side of the busy main road, to the
pavement in front of The Windermere Hotel. Now turn left (W) along
the A591 for a few metres until, just after you draw level with the bank
on the other side of the road, you see a lane heading up to the right,
clearly signposted to Orrest Head. Follow this, ignoring a path off to
the left early on.

2. The lane winds gently uphill through the trees. Soon after the
asphalt ends, the track forks at a bench. Bear right here. Continue
uphill and go through a metal kissing gate to gain the steps that lead
to the summit of Orrest Head.

It was on Orrest Head that guidebook writer Wainwright first fell in love with the Lake District. Fresh from his native Blackburn, he stood and looked out over the Coniston Fells, Crinkle Crags, Bow Fell and Scafell Pike and declared that what he saw was a "fascinating paradise". There are some superb views of the surrounding fells from here – too many to list. Simply choose your bench – there are quite a few – and sit back and soak it all up.

3. From the top, pick up the grassy path heading slightly east of north. Don't go through the next gate; instead, cross the stone stile in the wall to the right of it and then continue in a NE direction along a faint, grassy trail.

4. Keeping to the right of the wall at all times, you will eventually reach a minor road. Turn right here and walk along the road for about 340 metres, ignoring the first footpath on the left, close to the buildings at Near Orrest. Keep going for another 130 metres and then cross the stile in the wall on your left – signposted Moor Howe.

5. There is no path on the ground across the next couple of fields. Head NNE, straight towards the pole in the middle of the field and then continue up to and over a ladder stile. Maintaining the same NNE line, cross this field to exit it via a wooden gate – the left of two gates in the top wall. Now cross to the ladder stile over to your right. Beyond this, turn left to walk with the wall on your left.

6. Turn right along Moorhowe Road and follow it until you reach a clear, wide track on the left. This is Dubbs Road, which you now follow for 2.7km, passing Dubbs Reservoir on the way.

Dubbs Reservoir was originally constructed to supply Windermere, but then became an adjunct to the Thirlmere Aqueduct, serving Manchester. The reservoir and beck downstream provide important habitats for pearl mussels and crayfish.

Dubbs Reservoir

Orrest Head

Windermere

7. On reaching a junction with another track – the old Garburn Road – turn sharp left, reluctantly turning your back on the lovely view up the Trout Beck valley. When the track forks, bear left to head gently uphill. As the track begins to drop, the views are dominated by Windermere stretching on into the distance.

8. The track ends at a road, where you turn right. Then, in 120 metres, turn left through a gate – signposted Far Orrest.

9. Follow the grassy track south and then, as it approaches some trees, go through the left of two gates. Walk with a wall on the right until you reach a kissing-gate, which gives you access to a grassy lane between two drystone walls.

10. Approaching the buildings at Far Orrest, go through the gate on your right. Head west and drop to a gate. Once through this, cross diagonally to the right and go through a small gate.

11. The track goes through a gate and then heads up to and over a ladder stile. Head SSW towards a gap in the wall, but don't go through the gap; instead, bear left to walk with the wall on your right. Cross one stone stile, followed soon after by a ladder stile. Go through the next large metal gate and on to a track to the left of a pretty white cottage.

12. When you reach the road, turn right. At the junction with the A592, go through the old metal gate to the left. When the gravel track swings left, bear right along a narrower path that soon reaches a vehicle track. Go straight over – signposted Windermere and Orrest Head.

13. You now go through a rusty gate before crossing a footbridge and then climbing. When you reach Elleray Bank's surfaced driveway, go straight across. Pass to the left of some buildings belonging to St Anne's School and ignore the next track on your left.

14. Eventually, you will come out on to the lane that you took up to Orrest Head at the start of the walk. Turn right and then left along the main road to retrace your steps to the railway station.

Before the railway was opened in 1848, Windermere was just a tiny hamlet called Birthwaite. The coming of the railways to the Lake District was much opposed by Wordsworth, who feared the "influx of strangers" would destroy the area's tranquility and threaten the morals of local people. His protests, and those of other conservationists and local landowners, didn't stop the railway, but they prevented it from reaching the lake itself, and the line was terminated at said Birthwaite, almost a mile from the lakeshore. In an attempt to draw tourists to this tiny, unknown place, it was renamed – and the town of Windermere was born.

Attempts in the 1870s to extend the railway line from Windermere to Keswick foundered because of cost. But the extension northwards had been vigorously opposed by campaigners who included the social critic and artist John Ruskin. Speaking of the potential tourists and fearing their moral character, he said: "I do not wish them to see Helvellyn when they are drunk."

JOHN RUSKIN

Like Beatrix Potter, Ruskin's love affair with the Lakes was the result of childhood holidays. He once said: "The first thing which I remember as an event in my life was being taken by my nurse to the brow of Friar's Crag on Derwentwater."

His first visit to the Lakes from his family home in the south-east was when he was five years old, and, 47 years later, he moved into Brantwood on the shores of Coniston Water. Although he described it as dismal and dilapidated at the time, he bought it for its views – paying £1,500 for the privilege. He lived there until he died in 1900 – at the age of 80.

A writer, art historian, social critic and conservationist, Ruskin's theories about social justice influenced the development of the Labour Party and were frequently quoted by Mahatma Gandhi. Tolstoy described him as "one of the most remarkable men, not only of England and our time but of all countries and all times. He was one of those rare men who think with their hearts". He was also influential in the setting up of the National Trust, introducing two of the co-founders – Hardwicke Rawnsley and Octavia Hill – to each other in 1875.

Although he wrote many pamphlets aimed at the "working men of England" and taught at the Working Men's College in London, like Wordsworth, he wasn't keen to share his beloved Lakes with the masses, calling them "stupid herds of modern tourists".

9

HELM CRAG

Helm Crag (405m) sits above the village of Grasmere, its summit rocks attracting the attention of motorists as they drive along the A591. The highest rocks, known as the Howitzer, are clearly identifiable as you come down from Dunmail Raise. The Lion and The Lamb, on the other hand, are best seen on the journey up from the south.

This short walk ascends the well-used path from the Easedale end of Grasmere. The short summit ridge is an amazing collection of jagged pinnacles and shattered crags. The highest point – the infamous Howitzer – can be easily avoided in you don't fancy the scramble. The route then drops down a steep, grassy slope on the NE side of the hause between Helm Crag and Gibson Knott.
There is some road walking involved, but most of this is on quiet lanes – apart from a short section along the busy A591.

Start/Finish: Layby on A591, almost 2km south of Dunmail Raise and 700 metres north of the Traveller's Rest pub (NY335096)
Distance: 5.8km (3.6 miles)
Height gain: 376m (1,234ft)

---

1. The most dangerous bit on this walk comes as soon as you leave your car – you need to cross the road. Please be extremely careful because the traffic moves very fast here, well in excess of the speed limit at times. Once you're safely across and on the narrow grass strip on the other side, turn right and head uphill. Take the next turning on your left, towards Townhead.

> *There used to be a toll gate at Townhead on the old road between Keswick and Ambleside. The route, which*

had been one of the few 'roads' in the area before the Turnpike Act was passed in 1663, became a turnpike in 1761. The act allowed magistrates, and later private companies, to charge people for using roads – via tollgates. The money raised was spent on properly maintaining them. Many travellers objected to paying road tolls and would jump over toll gates to avoid the fee. To discourage this, spikes (or pikes) were placed at the top of the gates - hence the name turnpike.

2. The road winds through the first group of buildings and down to Ghyll Foot, where you will see a turning on your right to Greenburn. Ignore this for now; this is where you will re-emerge at the end of the walk. Having walked along the quiet lane for almost 1km, you come to a fork at a confluence of becks. Bear right here. A few minutes after passing the farm at Underhelm, turn right along the track to Thorney How Youth Hostel. You pass the hostel on your left and then cross straight over the driveway to Lancrigg Country House Hotel.

3. Turn right at the T-junction – along a very quiet lane. When this forks, bear right – towards Far Easedale and Helm Crag. Head up the walled track and through the gate at the top. Turn right in a few metres – signposted Helm Crag – and, when this narrower, walled track ends, right again.

4. The route ahead appears to split in three; you want the one furthest left, a well-walked, stony path heading uphill. Stick to this clear, steep path as it winds its way up the fell, passing some disused quarry workings early on before leaving the trees behind and encountering more open, but still craggy fellside.

When you reach the first open terrace, you find yourself looking up Easedale with the white streak of Sourmilk Gill slicing through the bedrock to the west.

5. Eventually, the pitched path runs out and, as you reach an area of

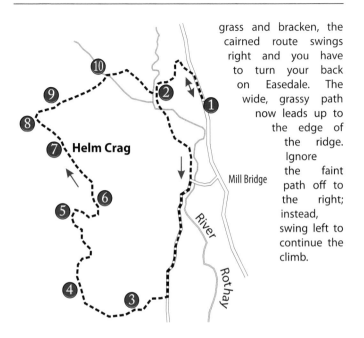

grass and bracken, the cairned route swings right and you have to turn your back on Easedale. The wide, grassy path now leads up to the edge of the ridge. Ignore the faint path off to the right; instead, swing left to continue the climb.

6. Clambering upwards, you soon encounter a fork in the path. The left-hand route is the easier option, missing out the straightforward scrambling up to the Lion and the Lamb. The right-hand option is preferable because it gives you a chance to look down on the fascinating jumble of shattered rocks to the east of the ridge. The last few metres of slippery rock to gain the top of the Lion can be easily avoided.

7. Beyond this first group of rocks, the paths converge for the final climb towards the highest rocks on the ridge – the so-called Howitzer. The true summit is reached only by a tricky scramble on the bare rock. If you do attempt it, be warned – coming down is much harder and potentially more dangerous than going up.

Helm Crag is just one of 214 Wainwrights – the fells listed in the guidebook writer's famous Pictorial Guide to the Lakeland Fells series. It is, however, the one peak which defeated him. In The Central Fells, the third volume of the series, he described the Howitzer as "a pinnacle of rock airily thrust out above a dark abyss... not to be attained by walking... brought underfoot only by precarious manoeuvres of the body". In his description of Helm Crag, he left a small space surrounded by dotted lines with a note saying: "This corner was reserved for an announcement that the author had succeeded in surmounting the highest point. Up to the time of going to press, however, such an announcement cannot be made." The space remained empty.

8. The ridge path continues in a NW direction. It is a little hard to spot the route from the top, but there are cairns to guide you. At the bottom of the slope, watch for a tiny cairn to the right of the path. This marks the top of a narrow path heading steeply down through the bracken – your route off the fell. Further down, the path gets even steeper. Watch your footing here because the short, cropped grass gets slippery in damp or icy conditions.

9. Cross the ladder stile in the drystone wall and continue down the grassy slope. As indicated by the waymarker on the post, keep fairly close to the wall on your left and don't be tempted by the faint path off to the right. Once through the gap in the wall corner, cross straight over to go through a small, wooden gate with a white waymarker on it. Now head for the beck, which you cross via a wooden footbridge.

10. At the top of the steps on the other side, turn right along the track. Go through the gate and, when the wall on your right ends, go through the gate over to the left. Turn right along the surfaced lane and then left at the T-junction. Now walk back up to the main road, along which you turn right to retrace your steps to the parking area.

10

WANSFELL PIKE

If it wasn't for the steep climb up on to Wansfell Pike (482m), this walk would simply be an easy afternoon's stroll – it includes a visit to a 90ft waterfall, pleasant green lanes, relaxing woodland paths, superb viewpoints and, as if all that wasn't enough, an interesting village complete with pub half way through the route. What more could you want? And that climb isn't so bad – before you know it, all your exertions are over and you're rewarded with great views of the surrounding fells and Windermere.

Start/Finish: Rydal Road car park in Ambleside,
just north of village centre on A591 (NY374047)
Distance: 10.3km (6.4 miles)
Height gain: 569m (1,866ft)

---

1. Use the pedestrian bridge near the toilet block to exit the car park. Turn right along the main road, bearing left and crossing over when the road forks. Pass the Salutation Hotel and turn left along a lane immediately after Barclays Bank. Turn left at the next lane where you will see a signpost to "The waterfalls".

> *Using the power of the mountain becks to good advantage, the people of Ambleside built many mills down the centuries. These included a bobbin mill, cotton mills, a cornmill and a paper mill. The area around Stock Ghyll alone had at least six mills.*

2. Follow this lane uphill until you come to a track on your left with a signpost reading: "This way to the waterfalls." Turn left here to follow

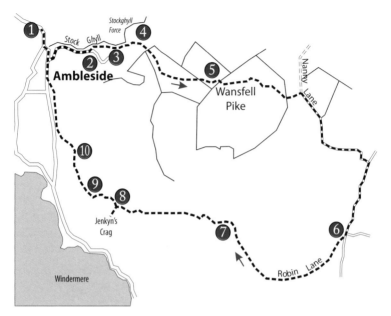

Stock Ghyll upstream. Red waymarkers indicate the way to the falls –
do not cross the beck.

> *The many bridges across Stock Ghyll – and the turnstile
> at the top of the path – were first built by the Victorians,
> always keen to draw tourists to areas of natural beauty.*

3. At the top of the falls, as you reach a junction of paths, turn right. A
sign points the way to a revolving gate. Go through the gate and turn
left along the lane.

4. About 150m after a cattle grid, you will see a stepped stile in the
wall to your right. Cross this and follow the surfaced path uphill and
through a gate in another wall. Beyond this gate, the path becomes a
steep, stony staircase, which leads all the way to Wansfell Pike.

Wansfell Pike isn't the highest point on the Wansfell ridge – this accolade actually belongs to a point 1.5km to the north – but it does afford some of the best views. As you stand on the rocky top, your gaze will inevitably be drawn south to Windermere, but look to the north-east and you will see the rolling ridge of Yoke, Ill Bell and Froswick, leading up towards High Street.

5. From the top, cross the stile and follow the obvious path heading away from the wall (east). You will eventually go through a kissing-gate and, soon after that, a metal gate on to a lane between two drystone walls. Turn right here. This old drove road, known as Nanny Lane, leads to Troutbeck. When you reach the road through the village, turn right.

The village of Troutbeck consists mostly of 17th and 18th century homes spread out along a 2.5km-long stretch of narrow road just above the valley bottom. One of the first buildings you encounter on entering Troutbeck from Nanny Lane is Hoggart's House, named after playwright Thomas Hogarth, who used to live here. "Auld Hoggart", as he was known, was the uncle of 18th century painter and cartoonist William Hogarth. He achieved some notoriety locally for his bawdy poems.

One of the most interesting properties in Troutbeck is Townend, a 17th century stone and slate house that belonged to a wealthy "statesman" farming family. It contains carved woodwork, books, papers, furniture and old domestic implements collected by the Browne family, who lived here from 1626 to 1943. It is now owned by the National Trust and is open to the public.

6. About 750m after entering the village, take the track off to the right immediately after the post office. This is Robin Lane. Climbing gently, you follow this for 1.2km – ignoring several tracks off to the left – until you come to a kissing-gate next to a large wooden gate to your left.

Go through the gate and follow the path downhill.

7. Turn right along the asphalt track and head uphill to High Skelghyll. Go through the farmyard and then keep to the mostly level bridleway, which soon enters Skelghyll Wood via a gate.

8. A little way into the woods, you will come to a sign on your left for Jenkyn's Crag. A very brief detour from the main route will take you out on to the rocks for a great view down Windermere.

9. Back on the main path again, soon after the Jenkyn's Crag sign, you reach a fork. Take either branch, although the one on the right is better underfoot. When the two routes meet up again, you will see a path off to the left; ignore this and keep to the broader trail as it crosses Stencher Beck (meaning stony stream).

10. When you reach an asphalt lane coming in from the right, bear left, heading downhill. At a T-junction, turn right and, when you reach the main road, right again, back into the centre of Ambleside. When you see the Salutation Hotel ahead, follow the road round to the left and then retrace your steps to the car park.

Other titles by
QUESTA PUBLISHING LIMITED

LAKE DISTRICT
WALKS WITH CHILDREN
Buttermere and the Vale of Lorton
Around Coniston
Borrowdale
Ullswater
Around Kendal
Around Windermere
South Lakeland

EASY RAMBLES
Around Keswick and Borrowdale
Around Ambleside and Grasmere
Around Eskdale
Around Wasdale
Around Ennerdale & Calder Valley
Around Dunnerdale
Around Coniston and Hawkshead
Around Patterdale and Ullswater
Around the Langdale Valleys

SHORT WALKS
In the Lake District

YORKSHIRE DALES
WALKS WITH CHILDREN
Wharfedale
Swaledale
Wensleydale
Malham and Airedale
Ribblesdale

PEAK DISTRICT
WALKS WITH CHILDREN
Dark Peak

PENNINES
SHORT WALKS
Eden Valley and North Pennines

All QUESTA titles are available from
27 Camwood, Clayton-le-Woods,
BAMBER BRIDGE, Lancashire PR5 8LA, by FAX to
0705 349 1743, or email to sales@questapublishing.co.uk

www.questapublishing.co.uk